Anchors of Faith

Walking with God Through Mental Illness, One Ordinary Day at a Time

Dr. Cindy H. Carr, D.Min. MACL

The Anchored Series

This book is published by **CHC Connect**.

All views and opinions expressed in this work are those of the author. Any errors or omissions are unintentional.

Printed in the United States of America
First Edition, 2026

ISBN: 978-1-971192-25-3

For permissions or inquiries, contact:
Cindy H. Carr
cindyhcarr@outlook.com
www.cindyhcarr.com

About the Anchors Series

The Anchors series exists to help people live steady in the face of mental illness through practical tools, clear language, and compassionate support.

Each diagnosis-specific volume offers a structured set of Anchors (principles + practices) tailored to a particular struggle.

- *Anchors of Bipolar Disorder*
- *Anchors of Major Depressive Disorder*
- *Anchors of PTSD*
- *Anchors of Anxiety*
- *Anchors of ADHD*

Anchors of Support is written for the people who walk alongside someone living with mental illness—family, friends, ministry leaders, and helpers.

Anchors of Faith is the spiritual companion across the whole series. It is designed for readers who want to walk with God day-to-day while also taking mental health seriously as a real clinical reality.

How to Use This Book

Anchors of Faith is designed to pair with every Anchors title—regardless of diagnosis. You can read it straight through, or you can use it as a spiritual companion alongside the Anchors book that fits your primary struggle (anxiety, panic disorder, trauma/PTSD, agoraphobia, or major depressive disorder).

Here are three simple ways to use this book:

- Option A — One Anchor per week: Read one chapter per week and practice the Anchor at the end of the chapter daily (or as often as you can).
- Option B — Match your season: Choose the chapter that fits what you're facing right now (fear, shame, relapse, isolation, fatigue) and work it for two weeks.
- Option C — Pairing plan: Read the matching chapter in your diagnosis-specific Anchors book, then read one chapter here that strengthens your spiritual steadiness for the same week.

If you are supporting someone else who lives with mental illness, consider pairing this book with Anchors of Support so that your care stays compassionate, wise, and sustainable.

Acknowledgments

Thank you to every reader who has had the courage to keep going in seasons you didn't choose. Thank you to clinicians, pastors, friends, spouses, families, and support people who learn how to love well without shame or pressure. And thank you to the God who meets us in the middle of the day-to-day—not only at the finish line.

Dedication

This book is dedicated to everyone who has the courage to show up every day—even when it is hard.

Living with mental illness carries a kind of shame and stigma that does not follow most other diagnoses. It brings polarization, misunderstanding, and judgment that are not earned and are not deserved. People are questioned, minimized, blamed, spiritualized, avoided, or treated as dangerous or weak—simply for having a brain that works differently.

That is not your fault.

Mental illness is not a failure of character, effort, or faith. It is not a lack of willpower. It is not moral weakness. It is not spiritual deficiency.

Mental illness is what happens when the brain functions differently in ways that disrupt thinking, emotion regulation, perception of safety, energy, motivation, memory, or daily functioning. These differences can be invisible, unpredictable, and deeply exhausting. And yet, the burden placed on those who live with them is often heavier than the illness itself.

The shame attached to mental illness is not natural. It is learned. It is systemic. It is reinforced by broken assumptions, broken language, and a society that struggles to make room for suffering it cannot neatly explain or quickly fix.

If you have been made to feel like your struggle disqualifies you—this book stands against that lie. If you have been told to try harder, pray harder, or hide better—this book stands with you instead. If you have carried the weight of showing up while also carrying shame—this book is for you.

You are not the problem. The system that misunderstands, minimizes, or moralizes your suffering is.

May these pages remind you that your courage counts, your effort matters, and your life has dignity—even on days when functioning takes everything you have.

Showing up is not small. Surviving is not weak. And you are not alone.

Table of Contents

Preface

This book is for the reader who wants a daily, practical way to walk with God while living with mental illness.

You will find repeated themes: presence over performance, wisdom over shame, connection over isolation, and faithful steps over heroic outcomes.

If your symptoms improve quickly, I am grateful. If they improve slowly, I am still grateful. If they come in waves, you are not disqualified.

Whatever your diagnosis, you are welcome here.

As you read, keep this posture: take what helps, repeat what stabilizes, and seek additional care when you need it.

A Prayer Before You Begin

God, meet the reader of these pages with gentleness and truth. Where there is shame, bring grace. Where there is fear, bring steadiness. Where there is isolation, bring safe support. Give wisdom for the next step and patience for the process. Help this book be a companion that points to You and strengthens daily faithfulness. Amen.

Chapter 1
God Is With You, Not Waiting for You to Be Better

Walking with God through mental illness, one ordinary day at a time.

Some people come to faith hoping it will make life calm. And sometimes, it does. There are seasons when symptoms ease, the mind clears, and strength returns like sunlight after a long winter.

But many people come to faith and discover something else: they love God, and their nervous system still alarms. They pray, and their thoughts still race. They worship, and their body still tightens. They believe, and depression still presses down. They trust, and trauma still flares. They do all the "right" things, and the day still turns hard.

If that is you, I want to start with the sentence that protects everything else in this book:

God is with you—right now—not waiting for you to be better.

This is not a sentimental statement. It is a stabilizing truth. Because one of the most painful burdens mental illness adds is the fear that you are spiritually disqualified when you are symptomatic.

When your mind is loud, it is easy to assume God is quiet. When your body is anxious, it is easy to assume you are unsafe with Him. When you can't concentrate, it is easy to assume you are failing. And when you are exhausted, it is easy to assume that rest is weakness.

But the God of Scripture is not a God who only walks with people when they are strong. He walks with people who are afraid, confused, grieving, doubting, and overwhelmed. He walks with people whose bodies shake. He walks with people who don't have words.

This book is not written to replace clinical care, therapy, medication management, or medical evaluation. It is written to sit beside your Anchors books and add one layer that many people need: a diagnosis-agnostic way to walk with God in the middle of symptoms—without turning faith into a performance contest.

If you are not faith-based, you do not need this book. But if you are—and if you've felt the collision between spiritual language and mental health reality—this book is for you.

The question behind the question

Most people do not ask, "Where is God?" as a theology assignment. They ask it in a moment of fear:

- in the grocery store when your chest tightens
- in bed when your mind won't turn off
- at work when your concentration breaks
- in church when your body feels unsafe
- in the car when panic rises
- on the couch when depression makes movement feel impossible

What you are often asking is not merely "Where is God?" but:

"Does God still want me when I'm like this?"

That question is not rebellion. It is vulnerability.

Mental illness can make you feel like your inner life is unreliable. So your brain tries to find something to explain it. And if you are a person of faith, your brain may reach for spiritual explanations first—sometimes wisely, sometimes harshly.

This is where many people get trapped: they interpret symptoms as spiritual verdicts.

They start measuring God's closeness by nervous-system calm, and they start measuring their faith by symptom control.

But faith is not symptom control. Faith is relational trust practiced in reality.

Faith is not a performance

Let's name a few quiet beliefs that can grow in faith communities and inside faithful people:

- "If my faith were stronger, I wouldn't feel this."
- "If I were more mature, I wouldn't struggle."
- "If I pray the right way, this will stop."
- "If I'm still symptomatic, I must be doing something wrong."

These beliefs sound like accountability. But they often function like condemnation. And condemnation does not stabilize a nervous system—it heats it.

The gospel does not teach that God draws near only after you have improved yourself. The gospel teaches that God drew near when we could not.

So if you are waiting to feel better before you feel welcome with God, you have the order backwards.

God's presence is not the prize at the end of the race. God's presence is the strength for the race.

Two truths you will hold at the same time

Throughout this book, you will hold two truths that protect you from extremes:

Truth 1: Mental illness is real, and symptoms are real.

This book will not minimize what you experience. Anxiety can feel like danger. Panic can feel like death. Trauma can make the present feel like the past. Depression can flatten meaning until you can't reach it. Agoraphobia can shrink life until your world feels smaller than it should. These are not "moods you should get over." They are patterns in the brain and nervous system that require care.

Truth 2: God is present in reality—not only in relief.

Some people experience healing that feels immediate. Some experience healing that looks like long-term management. Some experience healing that looks like reduced episodes over time. Some experience healing that looks like endurance, support, and deeper compassion. The shape may differ, but the promise remains: you are not abandoned in the process.

If you only hold Truth 1, you may drift into hopelessness. If you only hold Truth 2, you may drift into denial or pressure. Holding both creates stability: you treat symptoms honestly and you practice faith without shame.

What “God with you” looks like on a hard day

When people say, “God is with you,” it can sound like a poster. So let’s make it practical. On a hard day, God with you may look like:

- permission to tell the truth without fear of punishment
- a next step instead of a perfect plan
- comfort that does not require you to pretend
- strength to do the minimum wisely
- the right help in the right lane
- a gentle return after you spiral
- a friend who shows up when you cannot

God often works through means: through treatment, through wise clinicians, through medication when appropriate, through sleep, through rhythms, through community, through boundaries, through honest conversation, through small repeated practices.

If you grew up in a spiritual culture where “help” was treated like a weak substitute for prayer, let this be a freeing correction:

Receiving help is not competing with God. It is one way God cares for you.

A simple reframe for the days you feel far

Here is a sentence you will return to often:

Feeling far from God is not the same as being far from God.

Mental illness can change felt sense. It can change emotion. It can change concentration and motivation. It can change your ability to experience comfort.

If you are depressed, you may not feel pleasure—even in things you love. That does not mean love is gone. It means your system is impaired.

If you are anxious, you may not feel safe—even in safe places. That does not mean danger is present. It means your alarm is loud.

If you are traumatized, you may not feel present—even when you want to. That does not mean you are failing. It means your body is protecting you.

So when you can't feel God, do not make a verdict. Make a practice.

The Anchor practice

Anchor 1: God's presence is not a reward for stability. It is a promise in the storm.

Practice 1: The 30-second Presence Prayer

When your mind is hot, you do not need long language. Short is stronger.

Try this (out loud if you can):
"God, I am here.
I feel __________.
Be with me in this.
Show me the next wise step.
Hold me while it passes."

If you can't fill in the blank, use one word: "afraid," "tired," "numb," "angry," "confused."

Practice 2: The Non-Verdict Rule

Make this agreement with yourself:
"I will not decide what God thinks of me while my nervous system is flooding."

Flooded brains make permanent conclusions.
Anchored people postpone verdicts.

Practice 3: The Next Faithful Step

Ask one question:
"What is the next faithful step I can actually do today?"

Faithful does not mean heroic. Faithful might mean:
- take medication as prescribed
- eat something simple
- step outside for two minutes
- text one trusted person
- reschedule what you cannot carry
- attend the appointment

- use a grounding tool
- go to bed on purpose
- ask for help

Practice 4: The "With-God" sentence

Add this line to whatever you're doing:
"I can do this with God, not for God."

When your faith feels small

Some days your faith will feel like confidence. Some days your faith will feel like a thread.

A thread is still connection.

Jesus did not praise people for having dramatic faith feelings. He honored the people who came—trembling, desperate, uncertain—and reached anyway. In Scripture, a mustard seed matters not because it is impressive, but because it is alive.

So if all you can do today is whisper, "Help," that is not failure. That is prayer.

Legacy Takeaway

God is not waiting for you to be better before He is near. His presence is a promise in the storm. You are allowed to seek help, practice wisdom, and take small steps without turning symptoms into a spiritual verdict.

Next Step

Write one sentence you will use this week when symptoms rise. Choose one:

- "God is with me in this moment."
- "I will not make verdicts while I'm flooded."
- "My next faithful step is __________."
- "I can do this with God, not for God."

Put the sentence somewhere you will see it: notes app, mirror, Bible margin, or a sticky note on your nightstand.

Closing Prayer

God, I am tired of measuring Your presence by my stability. Teach me to live from Your nearness, not toward it. When my mind is loud and my body is unsettled, steady me. Give me wisdom to seek the right help, courage to take the next faithful step, and grace to stop condemning myself for symptoms. Walk with me today. Amen.

Chapter 2
Symptoms Are Not Sin

When your mind is loud, you need clarity—not accusations.

If you live with mental illness and you love God, there is one struggle that often hides behind the symptoms: spiritual shame.

Not the healthy kind of sorrow that moves you toward change, repair, and truth. Not conviction that restores relationship.

Spiritual shame is different. Shame says, "I am bad." Shame says, "God is tired of me." Shame says, "I should be over this by now."

And here is why shame is so dangerous for people living with anxiety, panic, trauma, agoraphobia, or depression: shame does not calm the nervous system. Shame intensifies it.

So before we go any further, we need a stabilizing distinction:

Mental illness symptoms are not the same thing as sin.

That sentence will not solve your whole story, but it will keep you from making the wrong conclusion in your hardest moments.

This chapter is not here to argue that spiritual life has no bearing on mental health. Many studies across decades have found that religion/spirituality can function as a protective factor for mental health for many people, and that spiritually integrated interventions can reduce symptoms in some contexts.1–3

At the same time, research also cautions that certain kinds of religious coping—especially feeling punished by God, abandoned by God, or trapped in condemnation—are associated with worse psychological outcomes.4

So the goal is not "more religion." The goal is wise, grace-shaped faith that supports healing rather than increasing fear.

Two kinds of spiritual language: one heals, one harms

Many believers were taught spiritual categories that were meant to help—but when mental illness enters the picture, those categories can get misapplied.

Here is a simple way to tell the difference:

Conviction draws you toward God

Conviction is specific. It is about something concrete. It leads to repair. It leaves you with hope.

Conviction sounds like: "I spoke harshly. I need to apologize."

Conviction produces movement toward life.

Condemnation drives you away from God

Condemnation is vague, global, and hopeless. It turns symptoms into a character verdict.

Condemnation sounds like: "I'm failing as a Christian. I'm disappointing God. I'm just broken."

Condemnation produces hiding, isolation, panic, and collapse.

Mental illness loves condemnation language because condemnation matches what symptoms already feel like: danger, threat, doom, and no way out.

Why symptoms get misread as spiritual failure

When your brain is flooded, it looks for meaning. When your body feels unsafe, it looks for a reason.

If you are a person of faith, your mind may reach for spiritual explanations first—because your faith matters to you, and because spiritual language is familiar.

But symptoms have their own "logic."

- Anxiety says: "Something is wrong. Find it."
- Panic says: "You're dying. Escape now."
- Trauma says: "The past is happening again. Protect yourself."
- Agoraphobia says: "Don't go. You'll be trapped."
- Depression says: "Nothing matters. Don't try."

None of those voices are moral assessments. They are alarm patterns.

A stressed nervous system can generate spiritual-sounding conclusions that feel true but are not true.

This is one reason the research field distinguishes between positive religious coping and negative religious coping.4 When faith is experienced as comfort, meaning, connection, and hope, it often supports resilience. When faith is experienced as punishment, rejection, or fear-driven control, it can amplify distress.4

“If I were closer to God, I wouldn’t feel this.”

Let’s address a sentence many sincere people carry:

“If I were closer to God, I wouldn’t be anxious.”

“If I were closer to God, I wouldn’t have panic.”

“If I were closer to God, trauma wouldn’t still affect me.”

“If I were closer to God, I wouldn’t be depressed.”

These sentences sound spiritual. But they often function as a self-attack.

A better, more honest sentence is this:

“I can be close to God and still have symptoms.”

There is room in Scripture for people who love God and still tremble. There is room for people who believe and still feel overwhelmed. There is room for people who obey and still need care.

And if you want an evidence-based reminder that your spiritual life and your clinical care can coexist: randomized trials and meta-analyses of religious/spiritual interventions suggest that, for many people who value faith, spiritually integrated care can provide additional symptom relief—especially for anxiety and sometimes for depression—when delivered in a responsible, structured way.2–3

That does not mean faith replaces treatment. It means faith can be one lane of support within treatment.

The "Symptoms vs. Sin" grid (a clarity tool)

When you're activated, you don't need a long debate. You need a quick grid.

Symptom statements (neutral, accurate)

- "My anxiety is predicting danger."
- "My panic system is spiking."
- "My trauma response is activated."
- "My depression is flattening motivation."
- "My nervous system is flooded."

Shame statements (accusing, global)

- "God must be disappointed in me."
- "I'm a bad Christian."
- "I should be past this."
- "I'm failing."

Here's the rule:

When your mind is flooded, do not let shame do theology.

Name the symptom. Refuse the verdict.

A pastoral note about repentance

Some readers worry that saying "symptoms are not sin" means we are excusing everything.

We are not.

You are still responsible for how you treat people. You are still responsible for honesty. You are still responsible for making amends when you cause harm.

But responsibility and shame are not the same thing.

Mental illness can increase irritability, withdrawal, avoidance, or numbness. Those may have relational impact. But the correct response is support, skills, boundaries, repair, and care—not condemnation.

This is why the best faith-based mental health support is both compassionate and practical: it helps you tell the truth, seek help, and take the next wise step—without turning your nervous system into a moral courtroom.

The Anchor practice

Anchor 2: Symptoms are signals in a stressed system, not a spiritual verdict.

Practice 1: Replace verdicts with symptom language (60 seconds)

Take the sentence you're hearing in your head and rewrite it.

Verdict: "God is tired of me."

Symptom statement: "My depression is telling me I'm rejected."

Verdict: "I'm failing."

Symptom statement: "My anxiety is demanding certainty and I don't have it."

Verdict: "I'm unsafe."

Symptom statement: "My trauma response is activated; my body is bracing."

You are not denying reality. You are naming it accurately.

Practice 2: The three-sentence return

When you notice condemnation, return with three sentences:

1) "God, You are here."

2) "My body is having symptoms."

3) "Help me take the next wise step without shame."

If you can only say one sentence, say: "Help me."

Practice 3: Bring faith into your treatment lane

If faith is important to you, consider one simple integration step:

- Tell your clinician, "My faith matters to me, and I want it to support my healing."

Many clients report wanting their spiritual beliefs respected and, when appropriate, integrated into care.5

This doesn't require a faith-based therapist. It requires a respectful conversation and clear boundaries.

Legacy Takeaway

Symptoms are not sin. Condemnation is not the voice you must follow. You can love God deeply and still experience anxiety, panic, trauma activation, avoidance, or depression. Your calling is not to perform peace—it is to practice faithfulness in reality, with wise help.

Next Step

Write one sentence that separates symptoms from verdicts. Use this template:

"I am experiencing __________ symptoms, and that is not a spiritual verdict. My next wise step is __________."

Put it where you can reach it on hard days.

Closing Prayer

God, I renounce condemnation. I am not on trial with You. Teach me to recognize symptoms without turning them into shame. Give me discernment to seek help, humility to accept support, and courage to take the next wise step. When my mind accuses me, anchor me in Your steadiness. Walk with me today. Amen.

Endnotes

1. Koenig, H. G. (2012). Religion, spirituality, and health: The research and clinical implications. ISRN Psychiatry, 2012, 278730. https://doi.org/10.5402/2012/278730

2. Gonçalves, J. P. B., Lucchetti, G., Menezes, P. R., & Vallada, H. (2015). Religious and spiritual interventions in mental health care: A systematic review and meta-analysis of randomized controlled clinical trials. Psychological Medicine, 45(14), 2937–2949. https://doi.org/10.1017/S0033291715001166

3. Aggarwal, S., Wright, J., Morgan, A., Patton, G., & Reavley, N. (2023). Religiosity and spirituality in the prevention and management of depression and anxiety in young people: A systematic review and meta-analysis. BMC Psychiatry, 23, 729. https://doi.org/10.1186/s12888-023-05091-2

4. Ano, G. G., & Vasconcelles, E. B. (2005). Religious coping and psychological adjustment to stress: A meta-analysis. Journal of Clinical Psychology, 61(4), 461–480. https://doi.org/10.1002/jclp.20049

5. Captari, L. E., Hook, J. N., Hoyt, W., Davis, D. E., McElroy-Heltzel, S. E., & Worthington, E. L., Jr. (2021). Current mental health clients' attitudes regarding religion and spirituality in treatment: A national survey. Religions, 12(6), 371. https://doi.org/10.3390/rel12060371

Chapter 3
Prayer When You Can't Pray

Because sometimes the most faithful thing you can do is stay connected in small ways.

Some days prayer feels natural. Words come. You sense warmth. You feel steadier when you finish.

Other days prayer feels like lifting a weight with numb hands.

You sit down and your mind won't settle. You try to focus and your thoughts scatter. You start to speak and nothing comes out that feels real. Or you are so depressed that even opening your mouth feels like too much.

On those days, many people don't just struggle to pray—they start judging themselves for struggling.

"If I were spiritually strong, this would be easier."

"If God were near, I would feel it."

"If I could pray the right way, I would get relief."

That is where faith can become heavy instead of helpful.

Let's reset what prayer is.

Prayer is not an audition.

Prayer is not a test you pass.

Prayer is not proof that your symptoms should stop.

Prayer is relationship—connection— practiced in reality.

And here is something both pastoral experience and research support: for many people who value faith, religion and spirituality can be associated with better mental health outcomes, and spiritually integrated approaches can add benefit when they are used wisely and responsibly.1–3

Notice the phrase "used wisely." The same research literature also warns that negative religious coping (feeling punished by God, abandoned by God, trapped in condemnation) is associated with worse adjustment.4

So in this chapter, we're not trying to force a "strong prayer life." We are building a gentle, sustainable way to stay connected to God—especially when symptoms are loud.

The problem is not that you can't pray

The problem is what you assume it means when you can't.

If your brain is flooded, concentration will be harder.

If you are traumatized, your body may brace against stillness.

If you are anxious, silence may feel like danger.

If you are depressed, motivation may disappear.

None of that means God is far.

It means your system is under strain.

Feeling unable to pray is not a spiritual verdict. It is a signal: "I need a smaller practice."

The smallest prayers in the Bible are still prayers

Many people think "real prayer" must be long, eloquent, focused, and emotionally sincere.

But Scripture is full of short prayers—sometimes only one word—spoken by people who were afraid, exhausted, and overwhelmed.

Some days your most honest prayer is simply:

"Help."

"Hold me."

"Stay."

"Mercy."

That counts.

Three kinds of prayer you can use in mental illness seasons

You do not need one style of prayer. You need options.

Here are three lanes that work across anxiety, panic, trauma, agoraphobia, and depression.

1) Breath prayer (for a hot nervous system)

When symptoms are high, long prayers can backfire because your brain can't hold them.

A breath prayer pairs one short phrase with your breathing.

Examples:

- Inhale: "God, be near." Exhale: "Hold me."
- Inhale: "Jesus, have mercy." Exhale: "Give me peace."
- Inhale: "Spirit of God." Exhale: "Steady me."

This is not "less spiritual." It is wise. It meets your body where it is.

2) Lament prayer (for grief, trauma, and honest pain)

Lament is not faithlessness. Lament is faithful honesty.

It tells the truth without pretending. It brings pain into relationship instead of isolation.

A simple lament structure:

1) God, this is what hurts.

2) This is what I'm afraid of.

3) This is what I need.

4) I am still here with You.

3) Liturgical prayer (for low focus or depression)

Sometimes the best prayer is a borrowed prayer.

Depression and trauma can steal words. Liturgical or written prayers give you language when you don't have it.

Reading a short prayer slowly is still prayer.

"Does prayer actually help?" (a grounded answer)

Prayer is not a lever that forces outcomes. But for many people, faith practices can shape meaning, hope, and coping—things that matter deeply in mental health.

Large reviews have found that religion/spirituality is often associated with greater well-being and, in many studies, lower risk of depression and anxiety—though results vary by population and by how faith is experienced.1

Systematic reviews and meta-analyses of spiritual/religious interventions in mental health care also suggest that spiritually integrated approaches can reduce symptoms in some settings, particularly when the person values faith and the intervention is structured.2–3

Importantly, patients frequently report wanting their spirituality respected and, when appropriate, integrated into treatment.5–6

So the question isn't, "Should I add faith or treatment?" The better question is:

"How do I let my faith support my treatment—without becoming shame?"

The Anchor practice

Anchor 3: Prayer is connection, not performance—especially on symptomatic days.

Practice 1: The 10-second prayer

Pick one phrase and repeat it three times.

- "God, help me."
- "God, be with me."

- “God, give me the next step.”
- “God, hold my mind steady.”

Do not evaluate how you feel afterward. Just stay connected.

Practice 2: The 60-second breath prayer

Set a timer for one minute.

Inhale slowly and pray one short phrase.

Exhale slowly and pray one short phrase.

Example: Inhale “You are here.” Exhale “I am not alone.”

Practice 3: The 3-minute ‘borrowed prayer’

On days you can’t form words, read this aloud slowly:

“God, I am here.
I feel overwhelmed.
I cannot carry today alone.
Give me wisdom for the next step.
Bring me the help I need.
Hold me steady. Amen.”

Practice 4: The ‘with treatment’ integration sentence

If you are in therapy or taking medication, add one sentence to your prayer:

"God, use every wise tool available to help me heal."

That one line keeps you from setting faith against care.

What to do when prayer becomes a trigger

Some people have religious trauma. Some people were shamed in spiritual settings. Some people were taught that anxiety was rebellion, depression was laziness, and trauma was weakness.

If prayer language has been used to hurt you, go gently.

Start with neutral connection language:

- "God, I'm here."
- "If You're near, meet me."
- "Help me be safe."

And if needed, choose practices that feel non-threatening: music, a single Psalm, a short written prayer, a walk while you speak quietly to God.

Legacy Takeaway

When you can't pray the way you want, you are not failing. Your nervous system is asking for a smaller practice. Prayer is connection, not performance. Tiny prayers still count, and your faith can support your healing when it is shaped by grace rather than condemnation.

Next Step

Choose one "hard-day prayer" and write it where you can reach it (notes app, nightstand, Bible margin).

Pick one:

- "God, help me."
- "God, be near."
- "Hold me steady."
- "Show me the next wise step."

Use it once a day for one week—especially when you don't feel like it.

Closing Prayer

God, teach me to stay connected to You in honest, doable ways. When my mind is loud, simplify my prayer. When my body is afraid, steady me. When my heart is heavy, carry me. Help me receive Your presence without performing. And give me wisdom to use every good support You provide—therapy, medication, community, rest, and truth—without shame. Amen.

Endnotes

1. Koenig, H. G. (2012). Religion, spirituality, and health: The research and clinical implications. ISRN Psychiatry, 2012, 278730. https://doi.org/10.5402/2012/278730

2. Gonçalves, J. P. B., Lucchetti, G., Menezes, P. R., & Vallada, H. (2015). Religious and spiritual interventions in mental health care: A systematic review and meta-analysis of randomized controlled clinical trials. Psychological Medicine, 45(14), 2937–2949. https://doi.org/10.1017/S0033291715001166

3. Aggarwal, S., Wright, J., Morgan, A., Patton, G., & Reavley, N. (2023). Religiosity and spirituality in the prevention and management of depression and anxiety in young people: A systematic review and meta-analysis. BMC Psychiatry, 23, 729. https://doi.org/10.1186/s12888-023-05091-2

4. Ano, G. G., & Vasconcelles, E. B. (2005). Religious coping and psychological adjustment to stress: A meta-analysis. Journal of Clinical Psychology, 61(4), 461–480. https://doi.org/10.1002/jclp.20049

5. Oxhandler, H. K., Pargament, K. I., Pearce, M. J., Vieten, C., & Moffatt, K. M. (2021). Current mental health clients' attitudes regarding religion and spirituality in treatment: A national survey. Religions, 12(6), 371. https://doi.org/10.3390/rel12060371

6. Rosmarin, D. H., Forester, B. P., Shassian, D. M., & Webb, C. A. (2015). Interest in spiritually integrated psychotherapy among acute psychiatric patients. Journal of Consulting and Clinical Psychology, 83(6), 1149–1153. https://doi.org/10.1037/ccp0000046

7. Koenig, H. G., Pearce, M. J., Nelson, B., Shaw, S. F., Robins, C. J., Daher, N. S., Cohen, H. J., Berk, L. S., Bellinger, D. L., Pargament, K. I., & others. (2015). Religious vs. conventional cognitive behavioral therapy for major depression in persons with chronic medical illness: A pilot randomized trial. Journal of Nervous and Mental Disease. (Advance online publication). https://pubmed.ncbi.nlm.nih.gov/25816046/

Chapter 4
Scripture When Your Mind Can't Focus

Because God's Word can be a lifeline without becoming a pressure point.

Many people who live with mental illness love the Bible—and still struggle to read it.

Not because they don't care. Not because they're lazy. Not because they're rebellious.

Because symptoms change what your brain can do.

Anxiety makes your attention scan for danger.

Panic makes your body demand escape.

Trauma can make stillness feel unsafe.

Depression can slow cognition and flatten motivation.

So if you open your Bible and the words won't land, that is not a spiritual verdict. It is a human reality: your system is strained.

And the moment your reading becomes a scoreboard—"If I was a good Christian, I could do this"—Scripture stops feeding you and starts accusing you.

This chapter is about receiving Scripture in ways that support healing rather than intensifying shame.

What Scripture is for (and what it is not)

Scripture is not a performance tool.

Scripture is not a test of maturity.

Scripture is not a punishment for having symptoms.

Scripture is God's voice of truth into real human life.

It comforts. It corrects. It anchors. It reminds. It strengthens. It reveals a God who meets people in weakness—not only after they become strong.

If you have ever felt pressure to "do your quiet time" as if the goal is to check a box, let this be a gentle reset:

The goal is not to finish pages. The goal is to stay connected.

Why "more reading" can backfire in mental illness seasons

When your nervous system is flooded, your brain's working memory is reduced. Long passages can feel like trying to drink from a firehose.

So the answer is not always "push harder." The answer is often "shrink the practice."

This is consistent with what we know about spiritually integrated mental health care: structured, doable spiritual practices can support coping and symptom reduction for people who value faith, but practices that increase guilt or condemnation can undermine well-being.1–3

Four ways to receive Scripture when you can't focus

These practices work across anxiety, panic, trauma, agoraphobia, and depression because they are built for the brain you have today—not the brain you wish you had.

1) The one-verse method (for low bandwidth days)

Choose one verse—one sentence— and stay there.

Read it slowly three times.

Then ask one question: "What is the truest thing God is saying to me right now?"

If your mind argues, don't debate it. Just return to the verse.

This is not avoidance. This is training.

2) The 'carry verse' (for anxious and panicky moments)

Pick one short verse you can carry into the day like a handrail.

Write it on a note card. Put it on your phone lock screen. Tape it near your bed.

Your carry verse is not for proving faith. It is for borrowing steadiness when you need it.

3) The Psalm lane (for trauma and grief)

Psalms give language to feelings many believers are afraid to admit: fear, anger, sorrow, confusion, exhaustion, and longing.

If you don't know where to start, start with one Psalm a day. Not for analysis—just for companionship.

4) The 'listen' lane (for depression, fatigue, and brain fog)

Some days your body can't sit and read—but you can listen.

Audio Scripture on a walk counts.

Listening in bed counts. One paragraph counts.

Connection is the goal, not a specific format.

A grounded note about meditation and repetition

Repeating a short passage slowly is not "emptying your mind." It is giving your mind a steady place to rest.

Across the broader mental health literature, repeated attention practices (like mindfulness meditation) have evidence for reducing depression and anxiety symptoms in some populations.4–5

For faith-based readers, religious or spiritually integrated interventions—often including Scripture reflection, prayer, or religiously integrated cognitive-behavioral strategies—have shown additional benefit in some trials and meta-analyses, particularly for anxiety and sometimes for depression, when delivered responsibly and aligned with the person's beliefs.2,6–7

The point is not to make Scripture a technique. The point is to receive Scripture as truth that reshapes the story your symptoms are telling.

The problem of "weapon verses"

Many people have been handed verses like weapons: used to silence pain, minimize symptoms, or shame them into pretending they are okay.

If Scripture has been used that way in your past, you may feel your body tighten even before you read.

That is understandable.

Here is a wise principle:

If a verse increases panic and shame, pause and seek a safer entry point—often the Psalms, the Gospels, or a simple reassurance of God's presence.

You are not dishonoring Scripture by reading it in a way that helps you heal. You are honoring God by refusing condemnation.

The Anchor practice

Anchor 4: Scripture is nourishment, not a homework assignment—especially on hard days.

Practice 1: The 90-second Scripture reset

1) Read one verse slowly.

2) Put your hand on your chest or stomach and take three slow breaths.

3) Say one sentence: "God, let this be true in me today."

That's it. Ninety seconds counts.

Practice 2: The 'truth over symptoms' rewrite

Write two sentences:

1) "My symptoms are saying __________."

2) "God's Word says __________."

Example:

1) "My anxiety says I'm unsafe."

2) "God's Word says He is with me and will give me wisdom for the next step."

Practice 3: Build a personal 'safe verses' list

Choose 5–10 short verses that consistently calm shame and increase steadiness. Keep them in one place (notes app or notecard). On hard days, read only those.

Practice 4: Bring Scripture into therapy (optional)

If you are working with a clinician and faith matters to you, you can say:

"I have a few Scriptures that help me. Can we use them as coping anchors when I'm flooded?"

Many clients want their spirituality respected and integrated into care when appropriate.3,8

Integration should reduce shame, not increase it.

Legacy Takeaway

Scripture is not a test you pass to prove you're okay with God. It is nourishment for real people in real pain. When your mind can't focus, shrink the practice. One verse counts. Listening counts. Psalms count. Your goal is connection—receiving truth without turning it into pressure.

Next Step

Choose one carry verse for this week.

Write it somewhere you'll see it daily.

Then practice the 90-second Scripture reset once a day—especially on days you don't feel like it.

Closing Prayer

God, make Your Word a refuge, not a burden. When my mind is scattered, meet me in small portions. When my body is afraid, steady me with truth. When shame tries to turn Scripture into accusation, remind me that You are gentle and near. Help me receive what I can today, and trust You for tomorrow. Amen.

Endnotes

1. Ano, G. G., & Vasconcelles, E. B. (2005). Religious coping and psychological adjustment to stress: A meta-analysis. Journal of Clinical Psychology, 61(4), 461–480. https://doi.org/10.1002/jclp.20049

2. Gonçalves, J. P. B., Lucchetti, G., Menezes, P. R., & Vallada, H. (2015). Religious and spiritual interventions in mental health care: A systematic review and meta-analysis of randomized controlled clinical trials. Psychological Medicine, 45(14), 2937–2949. https://doi.org/10.1017/S0033291715001166

3. Koenig, H. G. (2012). Religion, spirituality, and health: The research and clinical implications. ISRN Psychiatry, 2012, 278730. https://doi.org/10.5402/2012/278730

4. Zhang, Y., et al. (2024). Mindfulness-based intervention for hypertension patients with depression and/or anxiety in the community: A randomized controlled trial. Trials, 25, (Article 8139). https://doi.org/10.1186/s13063-024-08139-0

5. Huberty, J., et al. (2021). A mindfulness meditation mobile app improves depression and anxiety in adults with sleep disturbance: Analysis from a randomized controlled trial. PLOS ONE, 16(9), e0257478. https://doi.org/10.1371/journal.pone.0257478

6. Rosmarin, D. H., Pargament, K. I., Pirutinsky, S., & Mahoney, A. (2010). A randomized controlled evaluation of a spiritually integrated treatment for subclinical anxiety in the Jewish community, delivered via the Internet. Journal of Anxiety Disorders, 24(7), 799–808. https://doi.org/10.1016/j.janxdis.2010.05.014

7. Rosmarin, D. H., et al. (2014). A multifaith spiritually based intervention versus supportive therapy for generalized anxiety disorder: A pilot randomized controlled trial. Journal of Clinical Psychology, 70(9), 10.1002/jclp.22085. https://pubmed.ncbi.nlm.nih.gov/24114846/

8. Oxhandler, H. K., Pargament, K. I., Pearce, M. J., Vieten, C., & Moffatt, K. M. (2021). Current mental health clients' attitudes regarding religion and spirituality in treatment: A national survey. Religions, 12(6), 371. https://doi.org/10.3390/rel12060371

Chapter 5
Grace for the Body

God often cares for the mind through the body—and wisdom is not a lack of faith.

Many people living with mental illness carry an unspoken pressure:

"If I were really trusting God, I wouldn't need this much help."

Help can mean a therapist. A medication. A routine. A boundary. A nap. A doctor. A support plan.

And when faith is framed as "needing less," people start hiding their needs—or judging themselves for having them.

So let's name something early and clearly:

Needing support is not spiritual failure.

Using wise tools is not competing with God.

Taking care of your body is not a lesser form of faith.

Scripture does not present human bodies as irrelevant to spiritual life. It presents us as whole persons—body, mind, and spirit—loved by God and cared for by God in practical ways.

That is why this chapter is in this book. Because many spirals get worse not because people lack love for God, but because they are under-resourced in the body.

Why the body matters (especially with mental illness)

Mental illness is not "all in the body," and it is not "all in the mind." It is a whole-person experience.

Your nervous system, sleep, hormones, nutrition, medication response, stress load, and trauma history all influence how your mind feels and functions.

This is not merely opinion. A large body of research links sleep disturbance with mental health symptoms, including depression and anxiety, and shows that improving sleep can reduce distress.1–2

And when it comes to treatment, decades of clinical research support that evidence-based psychotherapy (such as CBT and trauma-focused therapies) and, when appropriate, medications can reduce symptoms and improve functioning for many people.3–5

For people who value faith, research also suggests that spirituality can be a meaningful protective factor and that spiritually integrated care can add benefit when it is responsible, structured, and aligned with the person's beliefs.6–7

Notice the pattern: the best care is often integrated—mind, body, relationships, and faith—without shame.

A pastoral correction: treatment is not a lack of trust

Some readers were taught that needing medication means they are "not surrendered." Some were told therapy is "worldly." Some were shamed for having symptoms at all.

If that is part of your story, let me offer a gentle correction:

God can heal through prayer. God can also heal through means.

God can comfort through Scripture. God can also comfort through community.

God can strengthen in worship. God can also strengthen through clinical wisdom.

Using the means God provides is not unbelief—it is stewardship.

Three stewardship lanes that stabilize many people

This chapter is not here to give medical advice. It is here to help you hold a wise posture toward your body, your treatment, and your faith.

1) Sleep: the first stability lever (without perfection)

When sleep is disrupted, anxiety tends to rise, mood tends to drop, and coping capacity shrinks.

Sleep doesn't solve everything. But lack of sleep makes everything harder.

Research has found that insomnia and sleep disturbance can increase risk for depression and are strongly associated with anxiety and distress.1

And effective sleep interventions (including cognitive behavioral therapy for insomnia, CBT-I) can significantly improve sleep and reduce related symptoms.2

Faith translation:

Going to bed on purpose is not weakness. It is wisdom.

A simple rule: protect your sleep before you try to fix your whole life.

2) Therapy: a place to practice truth without shame

Therapy is not a place where someone "talks you out of faith." At its best, therapy is a place where you learn skills, build insight, process pain, and practice new responses.

For anxiety and depression, CBT and related evidence-based therapies have strong research support.3

For trauma, trauma-focused therapies are widely recommended in clinical guidelines and have substantial evidence for reducing PTSD symptoms.4

Faith translation:

Therapy can be a way of cooperating with God's work in you—learning to tell the truth and live differently.

3) Medication: not a moral verdict

Medication is not a magic solution, and it is not right for every person.

But for many people, medication can reduce symptom intensity enough to make therapy, relationships, and spiritual practices more accessible.

Large-scale evidence reviews have found that antidepressant medications can be effective for many adults with major depressive disorder, and that responses vary by person and medication.5

Medication decisions are personal and should be made with a qualified prescriber who knows your history.

Faith translation:

If medication helps your brain become less flooded, that is not cheating. That is care.

The danger of "all-or-nothing" stewardship

Many believers swing between extremes:

- "If I can't do everything perfectly, I won't do anything."
- "If I still have symptoms, nothing is working."
- "If I need support, I must be failing."

Those are not spiritual thoughts. They are anxiety thoughts and shame thoughts.

Stewardship is not perfection. Stewardship is consistency.

How to bring faith into treatment responsibly

If faith is important to you, you can integrate it without turning therapy into a sermon and without turning church into a clinic.

Here are three healthy integration moves supported by research on client preferences and spiritually integrated care:

1) **Tell your clinician your faith matters to you.** Many clients want spirituality respected and, when appropriate, integrated into treatment.8

2) **Use faith as support, not pressure.** Positive religious coping (hope, meaning, connection) can support resilience, while negative religious coping (punishment, condemnation) can increase distress.9

3) **Ask for coordination when needed.** With your permission, some people benefit when pastoral care and clinical care communicate clear boundaries and shared goals (safety, stability, support).

The Anchor practice

Anchor 5: Caring for your body is a spiritual practice of stewardship, not a substitute for trusting God.

Practice 1: The 'body kindness' checklist (5 minutes)

On hard days, ask: "What does my body need for me to be stable enough to take the next step?"

Choose one or two:

- Water
- food with protein
- sunlight or fresh air
- a short walk
- medication as prescribed
- a shower
- a nap
- a bedtime boundary
- reduced caffeine
- a check-in text to a safe person

Small kindness to the body is often the doorway to clearer thinking.

Practice 2: The 'wise means' prayer (30 seconds)

"God, I trust You.
Use every wise means You provide—
rest, treatment, support, and truth—
to help me heal.
Help me receive care without shame. Amen."

Practice 3: The two-lane plan (10 minutes)

Write two lines you can follow when symptoms rise:

Spiritual lane: "When I'm flooded, I will pray one small prayer and refuse condemnation."

Body lane: "When I'm flooded, I will do one body-care step (food, water, sleep, meds, movement)."

Keep it simple. Make it doable.

Practice 4: The 'next appointment' courage step

If you have been avoiding care, take one step today:

- schedule the appointment
refill the prescription
ask about side effects
ask for a therapy referral
ask a trusted person to help you follow through

Courage is often one phone call.

Legacy Takeaway

God is not honored by your collapse. He is honored by your honesty and your wise care. Caring for your body is stewardship, not a lack of faith. Sleep, therapy, medication (when appropriate), boundaries, and support can be the means through which God stabilizes you so you can live, love, and heal.

Next Step

Pick one stability lever for the next seven days: sleep, therapy follow-through, or medication consistency (if prescribed).

Write one sentence: "This week, my stewardship focus is __________."

Tell one safe person so you're not carrying it alone.

Closing Prayer

God, help me live wisely in my body. Free me from shame about needing support. Give me discernment to seek the right care, courage to follow through, and patience for the process. Teach me to honor You by honoring the life and body You've given me. Meet me in the ordinary steps—sleep, treatment, boundaries, and community—and make them places of grace. Amen.

Endnotes

1. Baglioni, C., Battagliese, G., Feige, B., Spiegelhalder, K., Nissen, C., Voderholzer, U., Lombardo, C., & Riemann, D. (2011). Insomnia as a predictor of depression: A meta-analytic evaluation of longitudinal epidemiological studies. Sleep Medicine Reviews, 15(4), 247–258. https://doi.org/10.1016/j.smrv.2010.11.001

2. Trauer, J. M., Qian, M. Y., Doyle, J. S., Rajaratnam, S. M. W., & Cunnington, D. (2015). Cognitive behavioral therapy for chronic insomnia: A systematic review and meta-analysis. Annals of Internal Medicine, 163(3), 191–204. https://doi.org/10.7326/M14-2841

3. Hofmann, S. G., Asnaani, A., Vonk, I. J. J., Sawyer, A. T., & Fang, A. (2012). The efficacy of cognitive behavioral therapy: A review of meta-analyses. Cognitive Therapy and Research, 36, 427–440. https://doi.org/10.1007/s10608-012-9476-1

4. American Psychological Association. (2017). Clinical practice guideline for the treatment of posttraumatic stress disorder (PTSD) in adults. American Psychological Association.

5. Cipriani, A., Furukawa, T. A., Salanti, G., Chaimani, A., Atkinson, L. Z., Ogawa, Y., Leucht, S., Ruhe, H. G., Turner, E. H., Higgins, J. P. T., Egger, M., Takeshima, N., Hayasaka, Y., Imai, H., Shinohara, K., Tajika, A., Ioannidis, J. P. A., & Geddes, J. R. (2018). Comparative efficacy and acceptability of 21 antidepressant drugs for the acute treatment of adults with major depressive disorder: A systematic review and network meta-analysis. The Lancet, 391(10128), 1357–1366. https://doi.org/10.1016/S0140-6736(17)32802-7

6. Koenig, H. G. (2012). Religion, spirituality, and health: The research and clinical implications. ISRN Psychiatry, 2012, 278730. https://doi.org/10.5402/2012/278730

7. Gonçalves, J. P. B., Lucchetti, G., Menezes, P. R., & Vallada, H. (2015). Religious and spiritual interventions in mental health care: A systematic review and meta-analysis of randomized controlled clinical trials. Psychological Medicine, 45(14), 2937–2949. https://doi.org/10.1017/S0033291715001166

8. Oxhandler, H. K., Pargament, K. I., Pearce, M. J., Vieten, C., & Moffatt, K. M. (2021). Current mental health clients' attitudes regarding religion and spirituality in treatment: A national survey. Religions, 12(6), 371. https://doi.org/10.3390/rel12060371

9. Ano, G. G., & Vasconcelles, E. B. (2005). Religious coping and psychological adjustment to stress: A meta-analysis. Journal of Clinical Psychology, 61(4), 461–480. https://doi.org/10.1002/jclp.20049

Chapter 6
Lament Without Panic

Because honest sorrow is not the opposite of faith—it is often the doorway to it.

Some believers were taught that faith means staying positive.

That the spiritual goal is to "be okay," to "have joy," to "speak life," to keep the tone upbeat.

And when mental illness enters the story, that training can become a trap.

Because mental illness comes with real pain—fear, grief, loss, confusion, exhaustion, loneliness, and sometimes despair.

If you don't have a faithful way to tell the truth about pain, you will usually do one of two things:

1) You will stuff it until you snap, or

2) You will turn it inward and call it shame.

Lament is a third way.

Lament is not emotional chaos. Lament is not faithlessness. Lament is honest prayer that stays connected to God in the middle of pain.

Many people living with anxiety, panic, trauma, agoraphobia, or depression need lament because their inner world is already heavy—and pretending only makes it heavier.

The difference between lament and panic

At first glance, lament and panic can look similar: tears, fear, big feelings, and the sense that something is wrong.

But they move in different directions.

Panic escalates and isolates. It says, "This is unbearable. I'm alone. There is no way out."

Lament tells the truth and stays connected. It says, "This hurts. I'm afraid. God, meet me here."

Lament doesn't require you to feel calm. It requires you to bring your pain into relationship instead of into hiding.

Why lament supports mental health (a grounded note)

Pain that stays unspoken often intensifies.

Many mental health approaches recognize that naming experience—especially in a safe, structured way—can reduce internal pressure and improve coping.

For example, a large body of research on expressive writing and emotional disclosure suggests that structured, honest writing about stressful or traumatic experiences can have small-to-moderate benefits for health and well-being, with effects varying across people and contexts.1–2

Trauma-focused therapies also emphasize that healing often includes making meaning of what happened and reducing avoidance—at a pace that is safe and supported.3

For faith-based readers, the religious coping literature similarly distinguishes between coping that brings distress into connection with God and community versus coping that interprets distress as punishment, abandonment, or condemnation.4

Lament is the kind of faith practice that keeps you in connection.

You do not have to protect God from your feelings

One reason people avoid lament is that they think it is disrespectful.

They believe God can handle worship, but not anger.

That He can handle gratitude, but not fear.

That He can handle mature people, but not messy people.

But the Psalms tell a different story.

The Bible includes prayers that sound like:

"How long?"

"Why?"

"Where are You?"

"I'm afraid."

"This is too much."

God is not fragile.

You do not have to protect Him from your honest feelings.

Lament gives your suffering a safer place to go

When you do not have a faithful way to grieve, suffering goes somewhere else.

It goes into the body (tightness, insomnia, fatigue).

It goes into relationships (withdrawal, irritability, isolation).

It goes into the mind (rumination, obsession, despair).

Lament says: “Instead of letting this pain control me, I will bring it into God’s presence.”

That is not weakness. That is courage.

The four movements of lament (a simple structure)

Most lament in Scripture follows a pattern. You can use that pattern even if you don’t know what to say.

1) Address God

Start with connection.

“God…”

“Father…”

“Jesus…”

“Lord…”

2) Tell the truth

Name what hurts. Don’t polish it.

“I feel anxious and exhausted.”

“I’m scared my symptoms will never change.”

“I feel alone.”

"I'm triggered and I don't feel safe."

"I can't feel joy."

3) Ask for what you need

Be specific.

"Give me peace for the next hour."

"Help me sleep tonight."

"Help me take the next step."

"Bring me support."

"Help me tell the truth without shame."

4) Choose a tether (a small statement of trust)

This is not pretending everything is fine.

It is simply a tether that keeps you connected.

Examples:

- "I am still here with You."
- "Hold me while this passes."
- "I don't feel You, but I choose to stay."
- "Give me enough grace for today."

That's lament: connection, truth, request, tether.

Lament when depression is heavy

Depression can make prayer feel empty.

It can make words feel pointless.

It can make your body feel like it is moving through wet concrete.

If that is you, your lament might be only one sentence:

"God, I can't feel hope today—hold hope for me."

That is not weak faith. That is realistic faith.

Lament when anxiety and panic are loud

Anxiety and panic often demand certainty.

They push you to solve everything right now.

Lament helps by shifting the goal from certainty to connection.

Instead of "I must fix this," lament says, "I will stay with God through this."

Lament when trauma is activated

Trauma activation often makes the present feel like the past.

Your body may feel danger even when you are safe.

In trauma seasons, keep lament gentle and body-aware.

Your tether can be physical: hand on chest, feet on the floor, slow breathing.

Your words can be simple: "God, keep me safe right now."

The Anchor practice

Anchor 6: Lament brings pain into God's presence instead of turning pain into shame.

Practice 1: The 4-line lament (2 minutes)

Write or speak four lines:

1) "God, __________." (address)

2) "This is what hurts: __________." (truth)

3) "This is what I need: __________." (request)

4) "I will stay with You in this: __________." (tether)

Do not evaluate how you feel after. Lament is not a mood switch. It is a connection practice.

Practice 2: The 'name it, don't shame it' rule

When pain rises, repeat this sentence:

"I will name what I feel without turning it into condemnation."

Practice 3: Lament journaling (10 minutes, optional)

If you can, set a timer for ten minutes and write freely to God using the four movements above.

Research on expressive writing suggests that structured disclosure can help some people process stress and reduce internal load.1–2

If writing increases distress, stop and choose a smaller practice. Safety first.

Practice 4: Bring lament into support

Pick one safe person and say one honest sentence:

"I'm having a hard day. Can you sit with me, pray with me, or just check in?"

Connection is part of healing.

Legacy Takeaway

Lament is not a loss of faith. It is faith telling the truth. You do not have to pretend to be okay to be close to God. Lament gives your pain a place to go that is safer than shame and stronger than denial.

Next Step

Choose one hard situation you face regularly (bedtime, mornings, appointments, conflict, crowds, loneliness).

Write a 4-line lament for that situation and keep it where you can reach it.

Use it once this week—especially when you're tempted to pretend.

Closing Prayer

God, teach me honest faith. Help me tell the truth without panic and without shame. Meet me in my fear, my grief, and my exhaustion. Give me a tether when I feel untethered. Bring support where I am alone. And hold me steady as You heal me—through Your presence, through wise care, and through the people You send. Amen.

Endnotes

1. Frattaroli, J. (2006). Experimental disclosure and its moderators: A meta-analysis. Psychological Bulletin, 132(6), 823–865. https://doi.org/10.1037/0033-2909.132.6.823

2. Smyth, J. M. (1998). Written emotional expression: Effect sizes, outcome types, and moderating variables. Journal of Consulting and Clinical Psychology, 66(1), 174–184. https://doi.org/10.1037/0022-006X.66.1.174

3. American Psychological Association. (2017). Clinical practice guideline for the treatment of posttraumatic stress disorder (PTSD) in adults. American Psychological Association.

4. Ano, G. G., & Vasconcelles, E. B. (2005). Religious coping and psychological adjustment to stress: A meta-analysis. Journal of Clinical Psychology, 61(4), 461–480. https://doi.org/10.1002/jclp.20049

Chapter 7
The Shame Spiral and the Gospel

Because shame doesn't lead to healing—it leads to hiding. Grace leads to return.

Shame is one of the most common hidden companions of mental illness.

Not just the shame of symptoms, but the shame of needing help, the shame of having limits, the shame of "still struggling," the shame of feeling like you're disappointing God and exhausting other people.

And shame has a pattern.

It rarely announces itself as shame.

It usually shows up as thoughts that feel like "truth."

- "You should be over this by now."
- "You're too much."
- "You're a burden."
- "God must be disappointed."
- "You're failing."

That pattern is what I'm calling the shame spiral: a loop that takes a hard moment and turns it into a verdict about who you are—and about what God thinks of you.

This chapter is about interrupting that loop.

Not by pretending you're fine.

Not by arguing yourself into calm.

But by returning to the gospel: truth without condemnation, clarity without cruelty, grace that leads you back to God instead of away from Him.

Shame and conviction are not the same thing

People who care about doing the right thing are often vulnerable to shame because they mistake shame for spiritual maturity.

Here is the difference:

Conviction is specific and hopeful. It identifies something concrete and invites repair.

Shame is global and hopeless. It turns a moment into an identity and tries to end the relationship.

Conviction says, "You spoke harshly. Go make it right."

Shame says, "You're an awful person. Hide."

If you have mental illness, shame will often attach itself to symptoms:

"You had a panic attack. You're weak."

"You avoided the store again. You're pathetic."

"You can't get out of bed. You're lazy."

"You're triggered. You're broken."

Symptoms are hard. But shame makes them harder. (For the deeper reset on symptoms vs. condemnation, see Chapter 2.)

What research says about shame (and why it matters here)

Across the mental health literature, shame is associated with a range of negative outcomes, including higher psychological distress, depression, anxiety, and risk processes that keep people stuck.1–3

Shame tends to increase avoidance and withdrawal, which are also common maintenance patterns in anxiety, trauma responses, agoraphobia, and depression.4–5

In other words: shame doesn't just feel bad. Shame keeps you isolated from the very things that help: support, treatment, community, and honest connection.

For faith-based readers, the religious coping literature adds an important nuance: when people interpret suffering as punishment from God, abandonment by God, or evidence of spiritual failure, outcomes tend to be worse than when people experience their faith as comfort, meaning, connection, and hope.6

So if your "faith thoughts" are increasing shame and isolation, that is not spiritual growth. That is a signal to return to grace-shaped truth.

The shame spiral (how it works)

Most shame spirals follow a predictable path:

1) **A trigger happens.** A symptom spike, a setback, an argument, a hard memory, a sleepless night.

2) **A meaning gets attached.** "This means I'm failing."

3) **A verdict forms.** "I am bad. God is disappointed."

4) **Avoidance increases.** You stop praying, stop reaching out, stop attending, stop taking steps.

5) **Isolation grows.** The spiral tightens.

The trigger may be clinical, relational, or situational. The spiral is spiritual-emotional: it turns pain into condemnation.

A gospel reframe for the moment you want to hide

The gospel does not say, "Get yourself together and then come back."

It says, "Come back, and I will meet you."

Grace is not the denial of truth. Grace is the safest place to tell the truth.

So when shame says, "Hide," grace says, "Return."

When shame says, "You're out," grace says, "You're still held."

When shame says, "This proves you're not enough," grace says, "This proves you need help—and help is allowed."

Three lies shame tells in mental illness seasons

Lie 1: "My symptoms mean I'm spiritually failing."

Truth: Symptoms are signals in a stressed system. They are not a moral verdict. (See Anchor 2.)

Lie 2: "If I were mature, I wouldn't need help."

Truth: Maturity includes knowing your limits and seeking wise support. (See Anchor 5.)

Lie 3: "God is disappointed in me."

Truth: God's posture toward you is not driven by your symptom level. His posture is love. (See Anchor 1.)

The Anchor practice

Anchor 7: Shame is not a spiritual tool. Grace tells the truth and brings you back.

Practice 1: Name the shame out loud (10 seconds)

Shame loses power when it is named.

Say: "This is shame."

Or: "This is condemnation."

Or: "This is my illness talking in a spiritual tone."

Practice 2: The three-part interruption (60 seconds)

Use this script when the spiral starts:

1) **Name the trigger (facts only):** "My anxiety is high." / "I'm triggered." / "I didn't sleep."

2) **Refuse the verdict:** "This is not proof I'm failing."

3) **Choose return:** "God, I'm coming back to You right now."

Practice 3: Replace the hiding move with a connection move (2 minutes)

Shame will always push you to isolate.

Do one connection action instead:

- send a text to one safe person: "Hard moment. Can you pray or check in?"
- step into the light: "I'm not okay today."
- keep the appointment you want to cancel
- read one verse instead of none
- take medication as prescribed instead of skipping

This is where healing usually starts: not in heroic moments, but in small returns.

Practice 4: The 'grace sentence'

Choose one sentence you will use as a handrail:

- "I can tell the truth without being condemned."
- "God meets me in my weakness."
- "Shame wants me to hide; grace invites me back."
- "This is a hard day, not a spiritual verdict."

When shame is tangled with church experiences

Some readers have been spiritually wounded.

They were told their illness was rebellion or demonic.

They were pressured to stop medication.

They were shamed for boundaries.

They were blamed for trauma.

If that is part of your story, please hear this:

Being harmed by spiritual misuse does not mean God is unsafe.

It means people misrepresented Him.

If you need to rebuild trust slowly, that is allowed.

Start with safe practices: a Psalm, a short prayer, a trusted believer who is wise and kind, a counselor who respects your faith.

Legacy Takeaway

Shame does not produce healing. It produces hiding. The gospel produces return. When symptoms spike or setbacks happen, you do not have to turn the moment into a verdict. You can name shame, refuse condemnation, and take one small step back into connection—with God and with safe people.

Next Step

Write your personal shame spiral warning sign and your return step.

Warning sign: "When I start telling myself __________, I'm probably spiraling."

Return step: "When that happens, I will __________ (text a safe person / pray one sentence / read one verse / keep my appointment / do one body-care step)."

Put it somewhere you can see it.

Closing Prayer

God, expose shame for what it is. Help me refuse condemnation and return to You quickly. Give me courage to stay connected when I want to hide, wisdom to seek help without embarrassment, and grace to tell the truth about my symptoms without turning them into identity. Meet me in the spiral and lead me back to steady ground. Amen.

Endnotes

1. Kim, S., Thibodeau, R., & Jorgensen, R. S. (2011). Shame, guilt, and depressive symptoms: A meta-analytic review. Psychological Bulletin, 137(1), 68–96. https://doi.org/10.1037/a0021466

2. Tangney, J. P., Stuewig, J., & Mashek, D. J. (2007). Moral emotions and moral behavior. Annual Review of Psychology, 58, 345–372. https://doi.org/10.1146/annurev.psych.56.091103.070145

3. Cândea, D. M., & Szentágotai-Tătar, A. (2018). Shame-proneness, guilt-proneness and anxiety symptoms: A meta-analysis. Journal of Anxiety Disorders, 58, 78–106. https://doi.org/10.1016/j.janxdis.2018.07.005

4. Ehlers, A., & Clark, D. M. (2000). A cognitive model of posttraumatic stress disorder. Behaviour Research and Therapy, 38(4), 319–345. https://doi.org/10.1016/S0005-7967(99)00123-0

5. Abramowitz, J. S., Deacon, B. J., & Whiteside, S. P. H. (2019). Exposure therapy for anxiety: Principles and practice (2nd ed.). Guilford Press.

6. Ano, G. G., & Vasconcelles, E. B. (2005). Religious coping and psychological adjustment to stress: A meta-analysis. Journal of Clinical Psychology, 61(4), 461–480. https://doi.org/10.1002/jclp.20049

Chapter 8
Community Without Pressure

Because healing is rarely a solo project, and support should not require you to pretend.

One of the quiet lies mental illness tells is this:

"You should handle this on your own."

And one of the quiet lies shame adds is this:

"If you let people in, you'll be too much."

So people withdraw.

They smile and say they're fine.

They disappear from friendships.

They stop going to church or small group.

They cancel appointments.

They carry everything privately and call it strength.

But isolation is not strength. Isolation is a strategy your nervous system uses when it feels unsafe.

And while that strategy makes sense in the moment, it usually makes symptoms worse over time.

This chapter is about community—without pressure.

Not community as performance.

Not community as oversharing.

Not community as "tell everyone everything."

Community as wise support.

Community as safe connection.

Community as a place where you can be human without being judged.

Why community matters (what research supports)

Across decades of research, social support is consistently associated with better mental health outcomes and lower distress, while social isolation and loneliness are associated with higher risk for depression and anxiety.1–2

Support doesn't solve everything, but it changes the load you carry.

And for people living with mental illness, load matters: stress load, shame load, decision load, and emotional load.

For faith-based readers, community is not just a "helpful idea." It is part of how God often sustains people: through presence, encouragement, practical help, and shared burdens.

The fear: "If they really knew, they would leave"

Many people with anxiety, panic, trauma, agoraphobia, or depression carry a deeper fear than the symptoms themselves:

"If people really knew what it's like inside me, they would pull away."

Sometimes that fear comes from experience.

Sometimes you were misunderstood.

Sometimes someone said something careless.

Sometimes a spiritual leader blamed you.

Sometimes your family minimized you.

If that happened, your caution makes sense.

This chapter is not asking you to trust unsafe people.

It is inviting you to build safe support on purpose.

Three kinds of people: safe, kind-but-limited, and unsafe

Not everyone gets equal access to your inner world.

You do not have to treat every person like a safe person.

1) Safe people

These are people who can handle truth without panic.

They don't try to fix you quickly.

They don't shame you for symptoms.

They respect boundaries.

They can listen, pray, help, and stay steady.

2) Kind-but-limited people

These are good people who mean well but don't have capacity.

They might give unhelpful advice.

They might minimize because they're uncomfortable.

They might over-spiritualize because that's all they know.

You can still love them. But you don't have to hand them your hardest material.

3) Unsafe people

These are people who use your vulnerability against you.

They violate trust.

They shame you.

They pressure you to stop treatment.

They gossip.

They control.

With unsafe people, boundaries are not unkind. Boundaries are stewardship.

What community is not

Let's clear away a few myths:

Myth 1: Community means constant availability.

No. Sometimes stability requires limits.

Myth 2: Community means telling everyone everything.

No. Wisdom means discernment.

Myth 3: If I'm struggling, I shouldn't be around people.

Sometimes you do need rest and solitude. But chronic isolation usually increases symptoms.

Myth 4: If people loved me, they would know what to do.

People need clarity. Support improves when you ask for something specific.

How to ask for help without feeling exposed

Many people don't reach out because they don't know what to say.

So here are scripts you can borrow.

Script 1: The simple check-in

"I'm having a hard day. Can you check in with me later?"

Script 2: The prayer request with a boundary

"Can you pray for me? I don't want advice right now, just prayer and presence."

Script 3: The practical ask

"My symptoms are high. Could you help me with one thing—groceries, a ride, a call, or sitting with me?"

Script 4: The honesty-without-detail ask

"I'm not okay, but I'm safe. I could use encouragement."

These are not dramatic asks. These are stewardship asks.

The 'support menu' (a tool that reduces friction)

One reason people hesitate to help is that they don't know what would actually be helpful.

And one reason you hesitate to ask is that you don't want to be a burden.

A support menu solves both problems by making help clear and limited.

Create two lists:

What helps me (choose 5–10)

- a short check-in text
- sitting with me quietly
- a walk together
- prayer without advice
- reminding me to eat
- helping me get to an appointment
- watching the kids for one hour
- helping me clean one small area
- bringing a meal
- helping me leave the house for a short errand

What does not help me (choose 5–10)

- "Just calm down."
- "Just have more faith."

- "You're fine."
- unsolicited advice
- debate about my symptoms
- pressure to share details
- spiritual blame

This is not controlling people. It is guiding people.

Many supporters are grateful to have clarity—because they want to love you well.

Church and mental illness: a gentle way back

For some people, church has been life-giving.

For others, church has been complicated.

If church is hard for you right now, you have options:

- attend online
- attend for a shorter time
- sit near an exit
- attend with a safe person
- serve in a low-pressure way
- take a season to heal without guilt

Your relationship with God is not measured by your ability to handle a crowded room.

The Anchor practice

Anchor 8: You were not designed to carry mental illness alone—safe community is part of steady faith.

Practice 1: Identify two safe people (10 minutes)

Write down two names.

If you don't have two right now, write down one—and one place you could find a safe person (counselor, support group, wise mentor).

Practice 2: Send one low-pressure message (1 minute)

Text one safe person:

"Hard day. I'm safe, but I could use a check-in or prayer."

Practice 3: Build your support menu (15 minutes)

Write your 'helps' and 'doesn't help' lists.

Share them with one safe person.

Practice 4: The boundary sentence

Practice one sentence you can use when someone offers unhelpful help:

- "Thank you. What I need most is prayer and presence, not advice."
- "I appreciate you. I'm working with my clinician on this."
- "That doesn't help me. Here's what does…"

Boundaries protect connection. They don't destroy it.

Legacy Takeaway

You were not designed to carry mental illness alone. Safe community reduces isolation, increases resilience, and often improves coping. You don't need perfect people—you need a few safe people, clear asks, and boundaries that protect your healing. Community should not require you to pretend.

Next Step

Choose one:

1) Identify two safe people and tell them you're building a support plan, or

2) Create a one-page support menu and share it with one person, or

3) Re-enter community in a smaller way this week (short church visit, online service, one coffee with a safe friend).

Do one small step. Consistency matters more than intensity.

Closing Prayer

God, thank You that I was not designed to carry this alone. Give me wisdom to choose safe people, courage to ask for help, and humility to receive support without shame. Heal the places where I've been misunderstood or hurt. Teach me how to build community that is gentle, steady, and true. And use the people You provide—friends, family, counselors, mentors, church—to strengthen me as I heal. Amen.

Endnotes

1. Taylor, S. E. (2011). Social support: A review. In M. S. Friedman (Ed.), The Oxford handbook of health psychology. Oxford University Press.

2. Holt-Lunstad, J., Smith, T. B., Baker, M., Harris, T., & Stephenson, D. (2015). Loneliness and social isolation as risk factors for mortality: A meta-analytic review. Perspectives on Psychological Science, 10(2), 227–237. https://doi.org/10.1177/1745691614568352

3. Oxhandler, H. K., Pargament, K. I., Pearce, M. J., Vieten, C., & Moffatt, K. M. (2021). Current mental health clients' attitudes regarding religion and spirituality in treatment: A national survey. Religions, 12(6), 371. https://doi.org/10.3390/rel12060371

Chapter 9
Meaning Without Crushing

Because you are still called, even when your capacity is limited.

When mental illness is loud, one of the hardest questions is not, "How do I feel better?"

It is, "What is my life for now?"

Anxiety can make purpose feel like urgency.

Panic can make purpose feel impossible.

Trauma can make purpose feel unsafe.

Agoraphobia can make purpose feel out of reach.

Depression can make purpose feel meaningless.

And if you are a person of faith, you may carry a second layer of pressure:

"If I were really called by God, I would be doing more."

This chapter is about meaning—without crushing.

Because purpose can become either a healing anchor or a shame weapon, depending on how you hold it.

The danger of purpose-as-pressure

Many sincere people confuse purpose with performance.

They measure their value by output, their faith by activity, and their maturity by how much they can carry.

But mental illness exposes a truth we all need:

You are not infinite.

You have limits.

You were designed to need rest, support, and rhythms.

So when your capacity drops, the question is not, "How do I force myself back into my old pace?"

The question is:

"What does faithful purpose look like in this season?"

Meaning is not a mood

One of the crueler parts of depression is that it can flatten meaning.

Things that used to matter feel far away.

You can know something is important and still feel nothing.

That experience can lead people to scary conclusions:

"Maybe my faith is fake."

"Maybe I'm numb because God is done with me."

But emotional numbness is not spiritual abandonment.

It is often a symptom.

This is where it helps to remember: meaning is not the same as motivation.

You can live a meaningful life in a season where motivation is low.

What research says about meaning, purpose, and mental health

Across psychological research, a sense of meaning in life is commonly associated with better well-being and lower depression and anxiety symptoms.1–2

Meaning is also linked with resilience—the ability to keep moving through difficulty without losing your sense of identity and direction.2

For faith-based readers, spirituality and religious involvement are often pathways through which people make meaning, find hope, and experience community.3

And when faith is integrated in healthy ways, it can support coping—especially when it reduces shame and increases connection.4

Meaning doesn't erase symptoms. But it can reduce the sense that suffering is pointless—and that matters.

A pastoral reframe: calling is not always public

Many people imagine "calling" as something big, visible, and impressive.

But Scripture often shows calling as quiet faithfulness:

showing up, loving people, doing what is in front of you, practicing obedience in ordinary places.

In seasons of illness, your calling may look smaller than you expected.

Smaller does not mean less important.

It may simply mean more honest.

Three kinds of purpose that work in limited-capacity seasons

Purpose doesn't have to be one massive life mission.

In hard seasons, purpose often shows up in three lanes:

1) The purpose of healing (stewardship)

Sometimes the faithful assignment in a season is to heal.

To go to therapy.

To take medication consistently if prescribed.

To sleep.

To learn skills.

To create safety.

That is not selfish. That is stewardship.

2) The purpose of loving (small, real)

Mental illness can shrink your world, but love can still exist inside that smaller world.

Love can be one text message.

Love can be one honest conversation.

Love can be a boundary that prevents harm.

Love can be asking for help instead of collapsing.

3) The purpose of presence (with God)

Some seasons are about staying connected to God in the simplest ways: one prayer, one verse, one step.

Not because that is all you will ever do—because that is what is possible right now.

The 'minimum faithful life' (a freeing concept)

Many people measure themselves by their best days.

And then they condemn themselves on their worst days.

This book is inviting you to a different standard:

Define your minimum faithful life for this season.

Minimum does not mean "barely spiritual."

Minimum means "what I can do consistently without breaking."

For example:

- I will take my medication as prescribed (if prescribed).
- I will attend therapy (if in therapy).
- I will pray one sentence a day.
- I will eat two simple meals.
- I will ask for help when I'm flooded.
- I will take one short walk three times a week.
- I will stay connected to one safe person.

Your minimum faithful life is not a ceiling. It is a floor.

It keeps you steady when ambition, shame, or symptoms try to knock you over.

How to find meaning when you feel nothing

When you can't feel meaning, don't chase feelings first.

Chase actions that support meaning.

Small actions that often reconnect meaning:

- gratitude for one thing (not a list, one thing)
- service in a tiny form (send one encouraging text)
- creativity in a low-pressure way (music, drawing, writing)
- time in nature
- honest conversation
- spiritual practices that are small and safe (Anchor 3 and 4)

Across evidence-based approaches like Behavioral Activation, taking small meaningful actions can help counter depressive withdrawal over time.5

This is not pretending. This is rebuilding.

The Anchor practice

Anchor 9: Purpose is not pressure. God meets you in your capacity and calls you to faithful steps, not heroic outcomes.

Practice 1: Write your 'minimum faithful life' (15 minutes)

Complete this sentence:

"In this season, faithfulness for me looks like ___________."

Then write 5–7 items that are small, concrete, and realistic.

Practice 2: The 'today purpose' question (30 seconds)

Ask: "What is one meaningful thing I can do today within my capacity?"

Meaningful might be: take a shower, attend the appointment, reach out, rest on purpose, eat, pray one sentence, read one verse, take a short walk.

Practice 3: The 'no shame' boundary

Say out loud:

"My capacity is not my character. God meets me here."

Practice 4: Share your minimum with one safe person

Tell a trusted person:

"Here's what I'm trying to do consistently this season. Can you encourage me and help me stay steady?"

Connection increases follow-through.

Legacy Takeaway

Purpose is not pressure. God does not measure you by output; He meets you in your capacity. In seasons you didn't choose, your calling often looks like quiet faithfulness: healing, loving in small ways, and staying present with God. A minimum faithful life can keep you steady until capacity grows again.

Next Step

Write your minimum faithful life list and put it somewhere visible.

Then choose one item and do it today—without negotiating with shame.

Closing Prayer

God, free me from purpose-as-pressure. Teach me to live faithfully in the capacity I have today. Give me patience for the season I'm in, courage to do the next meaningful step, and grace to stop measuring my worth by output. Help me find meaning again—not through performance, but through Your presence and the small faithful life You invite me to live. Amen.

Endnotes

1. Martela, F., & Steger, M. F. (2016). The three meanings of meaning in life: Distinguishing coherence, purpose, and significance. The Journal of Positive Psychology, 11(5), 531–545. https://doi.org/10.1080/17439760.2015.1137623

2. Park, C. L. (2010). Making sense of the meaning literature: An integrative review of meaning making and its effects on adjustment to stressful life events. Psychological Bulletin, 136(2), 257–301. https://doi.org/10.1037/a0018301

3. Koenig, H. G. (2012). Religion, spirituality, and health: The research and clinical implications. ISRN Psychiatry, 2012, 278730. https://doi.org/10.5402/2012/278730

4. Ano, G. G., & Vasconcelles, E. B. (2005). Religious coping and psychological adjustment to stress: A meta-analysis. Journal of Clinical Psychology, 61(4), 461–480. https://doi.org/10.1002/jclp.20049

5. Cuijpers, P., van Straten, A., & Warmerdam, L. (2007). Behavioral activation treatments of depression: A meta-analysis. Clinical Psychology Review, 27(3), 318–326. https://doi.org/10.1016/j.cpr.2006.11.001

Chapter 10
When Symptoms Return

Because a flare-up is information, not a verdict—and not the end of your story.

One of the most discouraging moments in any mental health journey is the moment you thought you were "past it," and then symptoms returned.

You were doing better.

You were steady for a while.

You had a stretch of days where the fear was quieter, the sadness lifted, the intrusive memories calmed, or your world felt wider.

And then something happened—sometimes obvious, sometimes not—and the familiar weight returned.

In that moment, many people don't just feel symptoms.

They feel betrayal.

They feel panic about the future.

They feel shame.

They feel spiritual confusion.

"Was I ever really okay?"

"Did I lose my progress?"

"Did I do something wrong?"

"Is God disappointed?"

"Am I back at square one?"

This chapter is here to protect you from the most common lie that shows up in relapse:

“If symptoms came back, nothing changed.”

Symptoms returning does not mean you are starting over.

It means you are living in a body and brain that have patterns—and patterns can flare under stress.

Relapse is common (and it doesn’t erase growth)

In many conditions, symptom recurrence is a known part of the landscape.

For example, major depressive disorder often follows a recurrent course for many people, especially across multiple episodes.1–2

Anxiety disorders can also recur, and stress can amplify symptoms even after effective treatment.3

Trauma responses may reactivate under reminders or new stressors, even after significant healing work.

This isn't meant to discourage you.

It is meant to normalize what your nervous system already knows: progress is real, and recovery is often non-linear.

The faith collision: "I thought God healed me"

For faith-based readers, relapse can trigger a specific kind of spiritual grief:

"I prayed. I trusted. I felt better. Why am I here again?"

Sometimes people interpret that grief as spiritual failure.

But there is another way to interpret it:

You are learning to walk with God through a real human process.

Some people experience healing that is immediate and lasting.

Some people experience healing that is gradual and layered.

Some people experience healing that looks like management—fewer episodes, faster recovery, clearer support, wiser choices.

In all of those stories, God's presence is not conditional on symptom level.

The difference between a setback and a collapse

A setback is a rise in symptoms.

A collapse is when shame takes over and you stop returning to the things that help.

Symptoms are hard.

Shame makes them harder.

In Chapter 7 we named the shame spiral.

Relapse often tries to restart it:

Trigger → meaning → verdict → hiding → isolation → worsening symptoms.

This chapter is a return plan.

Not a perfect plan. A return plan.

What relapse is often trying to tell you

Relapse is not always random.

Often it is information.

Here are common contributors to flare-ups:

- sleep disruption
- increased stress load
- reduced support or increased isolation
- loss, conflict, or change
- anniversaries and trauma reminders
- medication changes or missed doses (if you are prescribed medication)
- decreased movement, sunlight, nutrition, or structure
- avoiding the very exposures or skills that keep fear from shrinking

Notice what is missing from that list: "God left."

Two questions that change relapse

1) "What is this asking me to return to?"

Relapse often calls you back to basics: sleep, skills, boundaries, support, therapy follow-through, medication consistency, prayer, Scripture, and honest conversation.

2) “What is the next wise step, not the whole solution?”

When symptoms return, your brain wants certainty.

It wants the whole plan, the whole timeline, the whole guarantee.

But healing rarely arrives as a guarantee.

Healing usually arrives as a series of small faithful steps.

Evidence-based relapse prevention (a hopeful note)

Relapse prevention is a real part of mental health care.

In depression, treatments like mindfulness-based cognitive therapy (MBCT) have evidence for reducing risk of depressive relapse for some people, especially those with recurrent depression.4–5

In anxiety disorders, continued skills practice, exposure principles (when appropriate), and maintenance strategies can reduce relapse risk and improve long-term outcomes.3,6

These findings reinforce a pastoral truth:

Stability is often built through ongoing practices, not one-time breakthroughs.

The Anchor practice

Anchor 10: A setback is not spiritual failure. It is a signal to return to wisdom, support, and grace.

Practice 1: The 'return list' (5 minutes)

Write five things that help you stabilize—your personal basics.

Examples:

- sleep boundary
- medication as prescribed (if prescribed)
- therapy session or coping skill practice
- one safe person to contact
- breath prayer (Anchor 3)
- one carry verse (Anchor 4)
- food + water
- a short walk or sunlight

Keep your list short. Make it usable when you're flooded.

Practice 2: The 'no starting over' statement (10 seconds)

Say out loud:

"This is a flare-up. I am not starting over. I am returning."

Practice 3: The relapse debrief (10 minutes, when you're calmer)

Answer three questions in writing:

1) "What changed before symptoms rose?"

2) "What supports did I lose or reduce?"

3) "What is one adjustment I can make this week?"

This turns relapse into learning rather than condemnation.

Practice 4: The early signal plan (15 minutes)

Relapse often has early signals: sleep changes, irritability, isolation, avoidance, racing thoughts, numbness, hopeless statements.

Write your top three early signals.

Then write your first response for each:

- "When I notice ___, I will ___."

Example: "When I start cancelling everything, I will tell one safe person and keep one appointment."

Practice 5: The 'treatment + faith' return prayer (30 seconds)

"God, I'm here again.
I refuse shame.
Give me wisdom for the next step.
Help me use every good support You provide.
Hold me steady while this passes. Amen."

When relapse feels spiritually confusing

Sometimes relapse triggers spiritual questions that feel scary:

"Did I do something wrong?"

"Is this punishment?"

"Why would God allow this again?"

If those questions come, you do not have to answer them in the heat.

Remember Anchor 1 and Anchor 2: do not let a flooded nervous system do theology.

Return first. Reflect later.

Legacy Takeaway

Relapse does not erase progress. Symptoms returning does not mean God is far, and it does not mean you are starting over. A setback is information: a signal to return to basics, rebuild support, and take the next wise step with God. Grace invites you back—again and again.

Next Step

Create your five-item return list and your three early warning signals today.

Share them with one safe person (or your clinician) so you're not carrying relapse alone.

Closing Prayer

God, when symptoms return, keep me from shame. Remind me that I am not starting over—I am returning. Give me clarity, courage, and patience. Help me rebuild the basics, reach for support, and take the next faithful step. Hold me steady through flare-ups, and teach me to live in grace while I heal. Amen.

Endnotes

1. Hardeveld, F., Spijker, J., De Graaf, R., Nolen, W. A., & Beekman, A. T. F. (2010). Recurrence of major depressive disorder and its predictors in the general population: Results from The Netherlands Mental Health Survey and Incidence Study (NEMESIS). Psychological Medicine, 40(10), 159–168. https://doi.org/10.1017/S0033291709991400

2. Solomon, D. A., Keller, M. B., Leon, A. C., Mueller, T. I., Lavori, P. W., Shea, M. T., Coryell, W., Warshaw, M., Turvey, C., Maser, J. D., & Endicott, J. (2000). Multiple recurrences of major depressive disorder. American Journal of Psychiatry, 157(2), 229–233. https://doi.org/10.1176/appi.ajp.157.2.229

3. Bruce, S. E., Yonkers, K. A., Otto, M. W., Eisen, J. L., Weisberg, R. B., Pagano, M., Shea, M. T., & Keller, M. B. (2005). Influence of psychiatric comorbidity on recovery and recurrence in generalized anxiety disorder, social phobia, and panic disorder: A 12-year prospective study. American Journal of Psychiatry, 162(6), 1179–1187. https://doi.org/10.1176/appi.ajp.162.6.1179

4. Kuyken, W., Warren, F. C., Taylor, R. S., Whalley, B., Crane, C., Bondolfi, G., Hayes, R., Huijbers, M., Ma, H., Schweizer, S., Segal, Z., Speckens, A., Teasdale, J. D., Van Heeringen, K., Williams, M., & Byford, S. (2016). Efficacy of mindfulness-based cognitive therapy in prevention of depressive relapse: An individual patient data meta-analysis from randomized trials. JAMA Psychiatry, 73(6), 565–574. https://doi.org/10.1001/jamapsychiatry.2016.0076

5. Teasdale, J. D., Segal, Z. V., Williams, J. M. G., Ridgeway, V. A., Soulsby, J. M., & Lau, M. A. (2000). Prevention of relapse/recurrence in major depression by mindfulness-based cognitive therapy. Journal of Consulting and Clinical Psychology, 68(4), 615–623. https://doi.org/10.1037/0022-006X.68.4.615

6. Craske, M. G., Treanor, M., Conway, C. C., Zbozinek, T., & Vervliet, B. (2014). Maximizing exposure therapy: An inhibitory learning approach. Behaviour Research and Therapy, 58, 10–23. https://doi.org/10.1016/j.brat.2014.04.006

Chapter 11
Spiritual Warfare Language

Because spiritual explanations can comfort—or they can crush—depending on how they're used.

Many faith-based people have heard the phrase "spiritual warfare."

And many people living with mental illness have wondered—quietly or loudly—what to do with that phrase.

Some people have been helped by spiritual warfare language.

It gave them courage. It reminded them they are not alone. It helped them resist despair.

Other people have been harmed by it.

They were told their anxiety was a demon.

They were told depression was rebellion.

They were told trauma symptoms meant they weren't surrendered.

They were pressured to stop medication or therapy and "just trust God."

They were blamed for not being healed.

So we need a wise, pastoral approach here—one that protects people living with mental illness and keeps faith from turning into fear.

Start with a stabilizing truth: mental illness is not a moral courtroom

Your symptoms are not proof that you are sinful.

Your diagnosis is not proof that you are under God's punishment.

Your need for therapy or medication is not proof that you "don't believe."

(If you need a fuller foundation for separating symptoms from spiritual condemnation, see Chapter 2.)

If spiritual warfare language is used to increase condemnation, it is misused.

Because condemnation does not heal. It isolates. (See Chapter 7.)

And as we've seen, shame and negative religious coping are associated with worse psychological outcomes.[1–2]

Two ditches to avoid

People often fall into one of two extremes:

Ditch 1: "Everything is spiritual warfare."

In this ditch, every symptom is interpreted as demonic activity.

Every intrusive thought is treated as possession.

Every depressive episode is framed as spiritual failure.

This can lead to fear, hypervigilance, self-blame, and avoidance of treatment.

It can also increase shame: "If I were holy enough, this would stop."

Ditch 2: "Nothing is spiritual."

In this ditch, faith is reduced to psychology only.

Prayer becomes optional or irrelevant.

Scripture becomes merely inspirational quotes.

This can lead to a different kind of poverty: spiritual disconnection, loss of meaning, and the absence of the comfort many believers need.

Wisdom avoids both ditches.

A wiser frame: both/and, not either/or

For many believers, it is reasonable to hold a both/and approach:

- You can take mental illness seriously as a clinical reality.
- You can also take spiritual life seriously as real and meaningful.

You can resist despair spiritually and treat symptoms clinically.

You can pray and go to therapy.

You can seek deliverance for what is spiritual and seek medication for what is biological or psychological.

This is not compromise. It is integration.

How to tell when spiritual warfare language is helping

Here are signs it is being used wisely:

- It increases hope, not panic.
- It increases connection to God, not fear of God.
- It leads to humility, not superiority.

- It encourages wise care (sleep, therapy, medication when appropriate, safety planning).
- It reduces shame and increases support.

If the language moves you toward God and toward wise action, it is likely helping.

Some Christians have experienced genuine encouragement through responsible warfare prayer; when it is practiced with humility and safety, it can strengthen hope—but it must never be used to shame symptoms, deny trauma, or replace medical and therapeutic care.

A constructive example:

A woman wakes up with panic symptoms—tight chest, racing thoughts, dread. In the past she would spiral into fear: "Something is attacking me; I'm failing; I'm unsafe." Now she uses a wiser frame. She says, "I will not partner with despair or condemnation today." She takes three slow breaths. She uses her coping plan. If she is prescribed medication, she takes it as directed. She asks one trusted friend to pray a simple prayer: "God, strengthen her and steady her." She takes a short walk and keeps her appointment.

That is spiritual resistance without spiritualizing. It treats fear like a real symptom and despair like a real enemy—while still using every wise support God provides.

How to tell when spiritual warfare language is harming

Here are warning signs:

- It increases shame: “This is happening because you’re not faithful enough.”
- It increases fear and obsession: “Everything is an attack.”
- It discourages treatment: “Therapy is worldly; medication is unbelief.”
- It blames the sufferer: “You opened a door.”
- It ignores trauma and the nervous system: “Just rebuke it.”

When people interpret suffering as punishment from God or abandonment by God—forms of negative religious coping—outcomes tend to be worse.2

So if your spiritual framework is increasing condemnation, it is time to adjust the framework.

A pastoral note about intrusive thoughts

Many Christians are terrified by intrusive thoughts because they assume a thought equals a desire—or a moral intention.

Intrusive thoughts are common in anxiety disorders and trauma responses, and they can be especially prominent in OCD-spectrum struggles.3

An intrusive thought is not a confession. It is not a prophecy. It is not a moral verdict.

It is often a symptom: an unwanted mental event that spikes distress.

Spiritually, you can treat intrusive thoughts with a wise combination:

- do not agree with them
- do not panic about them
- do not shame yourself for them
- return to truth and to skills (grounding, exposure principles, cognitive defusion)

A wise sentence for warfare without fear

Here is a sentence many readers need:

"I do not have to decide whether this is spiritual or clinical in the heat of the moment. I can take the next wise step either way."

If it's spiritual, wisdom still applies.

If it's clinical, faith still applies.

What to do when someone labels your illness as demonic

This happens more than people admit, and it can be devastating.

If someone says, "Your anxiety is a demon," you can respond with a boundary that keeps you safe:

- "I appreciate your concern. I'm receiving medical and therapeutic care, and I'm also praying. Please don't label my symptoms in ways that increase shame."
- "I'm not comfortable with that language. What helps me is prayer and support, not diagnosis."
- "My clinician and my doctor are helping me. I'm not stopping treatment."

Boundaries are not lack of faith. They are stewardship.

The Anchor practice

Anchor 11: Use spiritual warfare language to increase hope and wisdom, never to shame, deny, or replace care.

Practice 1: The three-lane response (90 seconds)

When symptoms rise, respond in three lanes:

Lane 1 — Body: "What does my body need right now?" (breath, water, food, sleep, meds as prescribed, grounding)

Lane 2 — Mind: "What is the symptom pattern?" (anxiety, panic, trauma activation, avoidance, depression)

Lane 3 — Spirit: "God, be with me. Give me wisdom. Help me resist fear and shame."

This keeps you from arguing about labels while you're flooded.

Practice 2: The 'no-condemnation filter'

Run every spiritual interpretation through this filter:

Does this interpretation lead me toward hope, humility, wise care, and connection?

Or does it lead me toward shame, fear, isolation, and denial?

If it leads to shame and isolation, reject it.

Practice 3: A prayer for warfare without fear

"God, protect my mind and heart. Give me discernment. Strengthen me to resist fear and despair. Help me use every wise support You provide. Keep me grounded in Your love. Amen."

Practice 4: Choose safe spiritual counsel

If you pursue deliverance prayer or spiritual counsel, choose leaders who:

- respect clinical care
- do not shame symptoms
- do not pressure you to stop medication
- prioritize safety and consent
- speak with humility

Legacy Takeaway

Spiritual warfare language can help when it increases hope, steadiness, and wise action. It harms when it increases fear, shame, denial, or pressure to abandon treatment. You can hold a both/and posture: treat mental illness clinically and resist despair spiritually—without turning your symptoms into a moral courtroom.

Next Step

Write your personal "both/and" statement for hard days. Use this template:

"Today, I will __________ (one clinical step) and __________ (one spiritual step) without shame."

Examples:

- "Today, I will take my medication as prescribed and pray one sentence."
- "Today, I will attend therapy and read one Psalm."
- "Today, I will practice grounding and ask God for wisdom."

Closing Prayer

God, give me discernment. Keep me from fear-driven spiritual explanations and from shame-driven conclusions. Help me resist despair without denying my symptoms. Teach me to walk in wisdom—using treatment, support, and spiritual practices together. Protect me from condemnation. Anchor me in Your love. Amen.

Endnotes

1. Kim, S., Thibodeau, R., & Jorgensen, R. S. (2011). Shame, guilt, and depressive symptoms: A meta-analytic review. Psychological Bulletin, 137(1), 68–96. https://doi.org/10.1037/a0021466

2. Ano, G. G., & Vasconcelles, E. B. (2005). Religious coping and psychological adjustment to stress: A meta-analysis. Journal of Clinical Psychology, 61(4), 461–480. https://doi.org/10.1002/jclp.20049

3. Abramowitz, J. S., McKay, D., & Storch, E. A. (Eds.). (2017). The Wiley handbook of obsessive compulsive disorders. Wiley.

Chapter 12
Long Obedience in the Same Direction

Because steady faith is often built in small steps, repeated—especially when the road is long.

Most people want a finish line.

A day when symptoms are gone for good.

A moment when the mind is calm, the body is steady, the past no longer flares, and the future feels safe.

And sometimes, that happens.

Some people experience healing that feels immediate.

Some people experience healing that becomes clear over time.

Some people experience long-term remission.

But many faithful people live another story:

Symptoms improve, then return.

Capacity grows, then shrinks under stress.

Hope rises, then dips.

Progress looks real—but it is not linear.

If that is you, you need a kind of faith that can live in a long season without becoming bitter, ashamed, or exhausted.

You need what I call long obedience in the same direction: a way of walking with God that does not depend on quick outcomes.

Faithfulness is not the same as feeling good

One of the most discouraging distortions in faith and mental health is the assumption that feeling better equals being closer to God.

It is possible to feel calm and be disconnected.

It is possible to feel distressed and be deeply connected.

Symptoms are not an accurate measure of spiritual closeness.

They are often measures of nervous system load, trauma activation, stress, sleep, hormones, and life context.

That doesn't mean your spiritual life doesn't matter.

It means your symptom level is not your scoreboard.

The role of patience in mental health recovery

Most evidence-based approaches to mental health care assume time.

Skills take repetition.

Exposure takes practice.

Trauma processing takes pacing.

Medication trials take patience.

Behavior change takes time.

Research across psychotherapy shows that treatments often work through repeated sessions and repeated practice—not one dramatic moment.1–2

And in chronic or recurrent conditions, maintenance strategies and relapse prevention practices matter.3

This aligns with a deeply biblical truth: growth is often gradual.

A mature definition of healing

Many people define healing as: “I no longer have symptoms.”

That is one possible form of healing, and we should never dismiss it.

But Scripture and lived experience show other forms of healing too:

- symptoms are less intense
- episodes are less frequent
- recovery time is shorter
- your support is stronger
- your coping is wiser
- your shame is lower
- your relationships are healthier
- your faith is steadier

That is not settling. That is growth.

The trap of outcome-based faith

When people believe, "God will love me more when I'm well," they live in pressure.

When people believe, "If I do everything right, I will never struggle again," they live in fear.

When people believe, "If I relapse, it means I failed," they live in shame.

Outcome-based faith turns God into a results manager.

It turns prayer into a transaction.

It turns your daily life into a test.

But the gospel is not transactional.

It is relational.

The steady practices that carry you

Most stability is built through small repeated practices—spiritual and clinical—done over time.

This is the same logic underneath recovery maintenance in many conditions: ongoing practice matters.3–4

Here are five practices that sustain long obedience in the same direction:

1) Return quickly (don't perform)

Your goal is not to never struggle.

Your goal is to return quickly when you do.

Return to God.

Return to your tools.

Return to your people.

Return to treatment.

Return to basics.

2) Keep your minimum faithful life (Anchor 9)

On hard days, you need a floor.

Your minimum faithful life keeps you steady until capacity rises again.

3) Practice "small and daily" instead of "big and occasional"

Small daily practices often outperform big occasional efforts.

One verse daily is better than a week of nothing and then an hour of guilt reading.

One sentence prayer daily is better than waiting for the perfect moment.

One weekly therapy skill practice is better than hoping insight will appear by itself.

4) Build relapse resilience (Anchor 10)

Flare-ups happen.

Resilience is learning how to return without shame.

Relapse prevention strategies are a meaningful part of long-term mental health care.3–4

5) Let community carry you (Anchor 8)

Long seasons require shared strength.

Support protects endurance.

When you are tired of the process

There will be days when you are tired of managing.

Tired of coping.

Tired of appointments.

Tired of doing the work.

If that is you, hear this clearly:

Being tired does not mean you are failing.

It means you are human.

On those days, your faithful step might be rest.

Or asking for help.

Or doing the minimum.

Or refusing to decide your whole future while you're exhausted.

The Anchor practice

Anchor 12: Faithfulness is not measured by symptom-free days but by steady return to God and wise practices over time.

Practice 1: The 'return rule' (10 seconds)

Say: "I return, not because I feel strong, but because God is faithful."

Practice 2: The 3-month view (2 minutes)

When you are discouraged, zoom out.

Ask: "What is one sign of growth in the last three months?"

Examples: fewer panic attacks, better boundaries, one more outing, faster recovery, less shame, more honesty, more support, better sleep rhythm, staying in therapy.

Your growth may be quiet—but it is real.

Practice 3: The endurance prayer

"God, give me grace for today—not the whole future. Help me take the next faithful step. Keep me steady in the long obedience. Amen."

Practice 4: The 'faithfulness over outcomes' statement

Write this sentence and keep it visible:

"My calling is faithfulness, not instant outcomes."

Legacy Takeaway

You do not have to live outcome-based faith. God is not waiting at the finish line; He is walking with you on the road. Healing may be immediate, gradual, or ongoing management—but in every version, faithfulness is the steady return: to God, to wise practices, to support, and to grace. Long obedience in the same direction is still obedience—and it matters.

Next Step

Choose one "small and daily" practice for the next 14 days:

- one sentence prayer
- one carry verse
- one sleep boundary
- one weekly connection with a safe person
- one therapy skill practice

Closing Prayer

God, I release outcome-based faith. Teach me to walk with You in steady steps. When I'm discouraged, remind me that progress is not always visible but it is still real. Give me patience for the process, courage to return when I drift, and grace to keep going when the road is long. Hold me in Your love, and help me live faithful today. Amen.

Endnotes

1. Cuijpers, P., Karyotaki, E., Reijnders, M., & Huibers, M. J. H. (2018). Who benefits from psychotherapies for adult depression? A meta-analytic update of the evidence. Cognitive Behaviour Therapy, 47(2), 91–106. https://doi.org/10.1080/16506073.2017.1420098

2. Hofmann, S. G., Asnaani, A., Vonk, I. J. J., Sawyer, A. T., & Fang, A. (2012). The efficacy of cognitive behavioral therapy: A review of meta-analyses. Cognitive Therapy and Research, 36, 427–440. https://doi.org/10.1007/s10608-012-9476-1

3. Kuyken, W., Warren, F. C., Taylor, R. S., Whalley, B., Crane, C., Bondolfi, G., Hayes, R., Huijbers, M., Ma, H., Schweizer, S., Segal, Z., Speckens, A., Teasdale, J. D., Van Heeringen, K., Williams, M., & Byford, S. (2016). Efficacy of mindfulness-based cognitive therapy in prevention of depressive relapse: An individual patient data meta-analysis from randomized trials. JAMA Psychiatry, 73(6), 565–574. https://doi.org/10.1001/jamapsychiatry.2016.0076

4. Craske, M. G., Treanor, M., Conway, C. C., Zbozinek, T., & Vervliet, B. (2014). Maximizing exposure therapy: An inhibitory learning approach. Behaviour Research and Therapy, 58, 10–23. https://doi.org/10.1016/j.brat.2014.04.006

About the Author

Cindy Carr is a pastoral counselor, writer, and advocate for compassionate, integrated mental health care within faith communities. She believes deeply in the presence and power of God, and she also believes in wise care: therapy, medication when appropriate, community support, and practical skills that help people function in real life.

Her work is shaped by a commitment to a *both/and* approach—one that honors faith without denying the nervous system, acknowledges spiritual life without moralizing illness, and invites people to walk with God through the ordinary, often nonlinear realities of mental health.

Cindy writes with a pastoral heart for those who love God and still struggle. Her goal is not to offer quick fixes, but to help readers build steadiness, reduce shame, and find language for faith that holds them in the day-to-day.

She believes showing up counts—even when it's hard—and that faithful living is often found not in dramatic outcomes, but in small, steady steps taken with honesty and support.

www.CindyHCarr.com

www.ingramcontent.com/pod-product-compliance
Lightning Source LLC
LaVergne TN
LVHW010949110826
845149LV00015B/3273

* 9 7 8 1 9 7 1 1 9 2 2 5 3 *